THE ICELANDIC
HORSE
A Breed Apart

TEXT:
KÁRI ARNÓRSSON

The Icelandic Horse
Text © Kári Arnórsson 1997
English translation: Sólveig Ólafsdóttir and Gary Wake
Photographs: Páll Stefánsson, except:
p. 37 and 38: Ragnar Axelsson
p. 45 Anna Fjóla Gísladóttir
p. 63 Dyre Fotografen
Assistance in photo selection: Audur Stefánsdóttir
Design: Erlingur Páll Ingvarsson
Lithography: Prentmyndastofan hf., Reykjavík
Printed in Italy
Published by Iceland Review © Reykjavík, Iceland 1997

ISBN 9979-51-122-2

Contents

As Old as the Nation

The horse arrived in Iceland with the Viking settlers and has made its mark on the land and the people since the earliest times of the country's settlement in the ninth century. Due to the island's isolation and an importation ban placed on other breeds, it can be thought of as being as well preserved as the Icelandic language, which has remained relatively unchanged through the centuries.

Today the Icelandic horse is adored by thousands of people who enjoy its company in their spare time. The increasing number of competitions being held, and the growth in exports of the horse have also resulted in a rise in employment in fields related to the Icelandic horse. Abroad it has numerous admirers, and in the last few decades it has been exported to countries throughout western Europe, as well as the North American continent.

Undoubtably, there is something quite special about this small breed, which hardly measures up to the riding horses familiar to those living in foreign lands – but only in terms of its size and shape, that is.

Since the earliest period of settlement the Icelandic horse has played a significant role in the life of the nation. In more recent times it has even been given a role in various movies.

STEED OF THE VIKINGS

As most of the people who arrived in Iceland during the settlement came from Norway, it is more than likely that the horse also originated from there, especially since Icelandic and Norwegian horses share a similar conformation among other distinctions. It is, however, impossible today to trace conclusively its origins to the breeds presently found in Norway. After its arrival in Iceland the horse probably mixed with horses from the British Isles.

The Vikings probably only brought with them the very best riding horses, stallions and breeding mares as it must have been very difficult to ship livestock on open boats across the rough seas.

Not only did the settlers bring horses with them, they also brought all the traditions and religious beliefs associated with the horse. In its new home the horse was still the chief's honour and his sceptre. No one else was allowed to touch it and those who did could expect to die. When a Viking died and his time came to join the warriors (Einherjar) in Valhalla, his horse was killed and buried with all its tack alongside its owner. Icelandic Sagas and finds unearthed in Iceland dating back to the Viking Age witness this custom.

Many of Iceland's highland pastures are impassable to all but those on horseback. The horse is still used to this day for the autumn sheep roundups.

An Indispensable Servant

Iceland is a fairly large island of 104,000km², but its people live mostly in coastal regions. It is safe to say that without the horse there would have been no settlement. It was the only means of transport for centuries and was not only ridden, but was used as a pack horse when people travelled from one farm or district to another, or across the highlands.

In those days people were unable to keep many horses, especially good riding horses. When the golden age of the nation (930-1262) passed, dark centuries of poverty, feuds and natural disasters ensued, and horses became a luxury few could afford. In a large, sparsely populated country the distances were long, with travellers often needing to cross the uncompromising highlands. Many had to walk, but those who were better off were able to traverse them on horseback.

A good riding horse has always been a source of joy to its owner. There were always some who kept brilliant riding horses specifically for that purpose. Indeed, it was considered prestigious and a sign of nobility to keep a horse for the pure pleasure of riding – good horses were highly valued and to this day occupy an esteemed position in the nation's literature. These horses were treated better than others, and it was often necessary to keep them shod in the wintertime in case the need arose to send for a doctor or a midwife. These trips were often taxing for the horses in snow and bad weather.

Old Traditions

Good riding horses, or gædingar as they are called in Icelandic, were always expensive, with good stud horses costing a fortune. Old stories relate that when a chieftain wanted to bestow an exceptional honour upon his friends, he gave them such horses as a gift, a gesture which was held in high regard.

The mounts of the chiefs and the heroes are often mentioned along with their owners in the sagas. Often the names describe the mounts, such as Gulltoppur (golden forelock), Léttfeti (one who treads lightly), Glær (probably a gray), Glaumur (the loud one), Gyllir (the golden one) and so forth. Many horse names became classic, with many of those deriving from old Norse religion and myths. For example, the high God of Norse mythology Odin rode a horse named Sleipnir across the skies. Sleipnir had eight legs and was sired by another deity.

Sigurdur Fáfnisbani (slayer of Fáfnir) rode the horse Grani when he slayed the worm and took all its gold as related in the Eddic poems, and as it says in *Hrafnkells saga*, Hrafnkell Freysgodi rode Faxi, the stallion the god Freyr gave him with the condition that anyone other than Hrafnkell riding the horse would die. These names are in wide use today.

But horses working just for their food had no such illustrious monikers. They were mostly named for their colouring, such as Raudur (chestnut), Brúnn

9

(black), Jarpur (bay), Gráni (grey), Bleikur (dun), Blesi (with a blaze), Stjarni (with a star), Skjóni (piebald/painted), Leistur (with one leg white), etc. Distinctive features in their looks or their personalities also contributed to their naming.

Today, names referring to a horse's markings or colour are uncommon although there are special instances which make obvious physical references: Skór (with one white hoof), Rák (with a white stripe on the nose), Glói (with a light mane and tail), Nótt (black as night), Logi (chestnut like fire), Blakkur (black), Lýsingur (palomino), Faxi (with dark mane), etc.

It is as common these days, as it has been throughout the centuries, to name horses for the farms where they were born. As a consequence it has almost become a rule that horses are recognized by their homes and are registered as such when they are shown: Glói frá Saudárkróki.

All exported Icelandic horses retain the place of birth in their names. It is also a tradition, which underlines the speciality of the breed, that Icelandic horses born on the mainland are given Icelandic names as well as the name of the farm: Glói von Wiesenhof.

ALTERED ROLE

It is difficult to say for sure how many horses have been in Iceland at any given point in time. However, it is likely that there has always been a considerable

A fluent trot. The horse always enjoys itself best when it is unbridled and free out in nature.

number, with the horse as much a part of the rural settings as sheep. In spite of this, no specific breeding of horses took place after Iceland's golden age – 930 to 1262 – until the 20th century. Most farmers only required horses that were suitable both for riding and harness – the quality of the gaits and the beauty of the horse were of little importance.

The horse has carried the nation throughout the centuries. When natural disasters and famine shrouded the population in the shadow of foreign occupation, the horse was as badly off as the people. Before the eruptions in Laki in southeast Iceland in 1783, there were believed to be around 36,000 horses in the country. After this natural disaster it was concluded that no less than 27,000 horses had been killed. Today, the horse stock in Iceland totals about 80,000, with roughly another 50,000 Icelandic horses in countries other than its homeland.

The role of the Icelandic horse has changed. Technology and machinery have usurped the working role of the horse at the farms. All that remains of its former role is its employment herding the sheep from the mountains in the autumn where they have been grazing throughout the summer.

These changes began in the 1940s and by the following decade horses were no longer used for farming. Admirers of the breed were concerned by this. They founded a union to protect the breed. The horse is generally regarded nowadays as a riding horse to be used for pleasure and enjoyment.

Riding clubs were founded throughout the country, and the breeding of riding horses became more organized. Stallions were chosen for their gaits and qualities as riding horses. As a result the National Association of Riding Clubs was founded and rules were agreed upon for breeding riding horses.

The horse has no less importance today than it had in earlier times. In the high-tech society we live in the horse is a source of enjoyment and relaxation to a growing number of people who long to be in touch with nature and treasure old traditions.

A Horse Unlike Any Other

The Icelandic horse is relatively small compared to the European horse breeds. It is only 132 cm high on the withers on average, but its conformation, training and various uses have all contributed to its enormous strength and endurance. Although it is more compact and has shorter legs than most other popular horse breeds, it is not classified as a pony, and no other horse breed has the same abilities as far as gait is concerned.

The Icelandic horse is most famous for the quality of its five gaits, but it is also renowned for its calm temperament. The horse is very amiable and easy to handle following its training and is thought of as a good companion who is willing to work. These are the characteristics which have made the Icelandic horse so popular both in its homeland and abroad.

FIVE GAITS

No horse breed in Europe has the same gaiting abilities as the five-gaited Icelandic horse. Besides walk (fet), trot (brokk) and canter (stökk), it has the tölt (running walk) and pace (skeid) which is characteristic for the Icelandic horse.

The most fascinating gait, the tölt (see photo p. 51), has been bred out of most of the larger breeds in Europe but can still be found in certain breeds in North and South America and in Asia. The tölt of the Icelandic horse is smooth but powerful. It is possible to ride a horse in tölt with varying speed, while carrying a full glass of beer – and without spilling a drop. The many tourists who annually visit Iceland on account of the horse are fascinated by its movements and its gaits.

In tölt the horse has the same footfall as in walk, except it is faster. Horses with good tölt can easily increase their speed from a really slow tölt to a tölt almost as fast as a gallop. The tölt is a four-beat gait and for a clear-gaited tölt the length between hoof beats must be the same.

Old men say that it is best to evaluate a foal's gaits seven or ten days after its birth. How a foal moves then will be an indication of how it will move when fully grown. Many horses only trot when moving freely and will not show tölt and/or pace until they are trained. Others show trot and tölt when chased around in the field, whereas others also show pace or move mainly in pace. In a few weeks and months their gaits may change under further influence of their environment. This can result in the young horse moving only in trot or in pace until it is trained in its fourth year. By then the owner knows what to expect from the animal when its training begins.

Sometimes the young horse only trots at the onset of its training – before long however, it starts to tölt without being pressed into it. Some young horses tölt as soon as they are ridden any faster than in walk, while others only want to pace. With a pacy horse the trainer has to work towards "clearing the gaits," which involves teaching the horse to drop the two-beat gait and use a clear four-beat instead.

Not all Icelandic horses have five gaits and a few of them are only three-gaited (walk, trot, canter). Many horses are four-gaited (the addition of tölt) while some also have a good pace.

The gaits of the Icelandic horse are like an instrument which requires tuning, even if a beginner can easily ride in a clear-beat and graceful tölt.

As Icelanders were mainly breeding horses for farming, they neglected the gaits, as they were of no importance for a draught horse. When they started to selectively breed riding horses early in the twentieth century, tölt became the main breeding goal and in terms of a horse's judging carries more weight than other gaits. All riders like to ride a clear-beat tölter who has a good carriage and high movements.

The demand for horses with fast tölt and high movements is gradually increasing and therefore the emphasis for these traits carries a greater significance in the breeding of the Icelandic horse. Many believe that a clear-beat, slow tölt should be the main feature of any good riding horse, as the slow tölt is the basis for smoothness and agility in the gait and in the horse itself. It is impressive to see a magnificent horse with high leg action and good movements ridden in slow tölt, so slow that its mane is barely moving.

Pace is a two-beat lateral gait where the horse moves the front foot and the hind foot on the same side at the same time (see photo p. 22). This gait enables speeds of up to 45 km per hour. Pace is only considered of quality when the horse is moving fast and powerfully. If the horse is moving slowly in pace it is called "piggy-pace" – a gait no rider wants to be seen using. Fast pacers have always been valued in Iceland and therefore both tölt and pace are referred to as "expensive" gaits. Pace is now only ridden at short distances. Special races in this gait have been held from the time of early settlement.

The tölt is difficult for the horse when used for long intervals and thus riders should only ask their horses for tölt when the ground is smooth and even. Trot is a relaxing gait for most horses and is the gait they mainly choose for themselves, especially when the ground is uneven and rough. It is considered a flaw in a horse if it does not trot when asked.

MANY COLOURS

The Icelandic horse is found in a greater variety of colours than most other horse breeds. This suggests that the horse has not been strictly bred, as controlled breeding tends to eventually produce few colours. It is interesting to note that with descriptions of horses presented in the old sagas their colour is often specifically mentioned; furthermore it would seem that the chieftains wanted all their horses to be of the same colour:

"And after the celebration Thorgeir gave great gifts. Finnbogi his nephew received five stud horses who were all of a yellow dun colour. It was said that this horse was the best horse in north Iceland and that of all Finnbogi possessed nothing was as precious to him as the stud horses. He often came to them and stroked them." (*Finnbogi rammi saga*).

The sagas reveal that good horses were valuable and loved by their owners, with great importance placed on their colouring.

The Icelandic horse is almost wild. Historically, it has been left to itself in the highlands where it has bred without human interference. This has of course changed in modern times, but is nonetheless one of the reasons for the colour variety in the breed. Rare colours are sought after and people are beginning to realize that this feature of the Icelandic horse should be protected and selectively bred.

The Icelandic horse stock features all the main colours with almost all the possible hues represented.

There are, however, some varieties similar to the Appaloosa spottings and the Knapstrup spottings which do not exist in the stock. The skew and piebald markings are different from those since the colour changes between the dark and the white patches are clearer than in the previously mentioned colours.

Altogether around one hundred varieties of colour are found in the Icelandic breed. Many of them are variations of the same basic colour. Thus, black is not one colour but consists of variations from pitch black to light brown, while in between there are several other shades. One colour variety is roan. Research has shown that horses of this hue change their colour throughout the year in four steps. These changes can occur in all of the basic colours and take place because the longer hairs are pigmented whereas the shorter hairs appear white but are in fact colourless. It is therefore the growth and length of the coat that leads to the colour variations – although the head and the legs always remain the same dark colour.

With selective breeding the colour variety has lessened although all colours are still found in the stock. The most successful stallions in the last few years have been black, chestnut and bay, and thus most of their offspring have these colourings. Most of the horses are now chestnut and black. It is striking how little there is of grey horses and of dun and painted horses.

Some breeders concentrate on achieving certain colours such as paints and silver dapples as horses with these markings tend to be much sought after by foreign buyers.

The colour variety in the Icelandic breed is a rare feature and contributes to the breed's popularity as well as being a pool of genetic wealth.

STABLED AND IN THE FIELD

In autumn the coat of the horse thickens, becoming quite furry. This hair growth enables the horse to withstand the cold and the wet. The horse also needs to fatten to survive a shortage in strength-producing food in winter. Icelandic horses prefer to be outside in winter providing they have shelter and enough to eat. The horses scrape the snow from the ground with their hoofs to get to the grass.

Today, horses are stabled earlier in winter than in previous times, and those which are not ridden during this time of year are fed outside. In regions of the country where the winters are not so harsh, foals are kept with their mothers outside almost until the spring. They learn to eat hay from their mothers, with many people believing this to be the best way for the horse to raise its young.

In other parts of the country foals are weaned from their mothers before the new year and stabled and fed. From that moment the foals are let out regularly as it is important that they get as much exercise as possible.

In Iceland it is usual for riding horses to be

turned loose in the autumn. From September until
December they roam freely in huge fields where
they regain their strength and freedom of spirit.
Around Christmas all horses that are going to be
ridden in winter are stabled. By June they are
turned out onto the grass again.

It is however, in the horse's nature to be raised
outside and not to be stabled during the long Icelandic winters. This outdoor life has contributed to
the individuality of the Icelandic horse. During the
summer months, horses were driven, where possible, into the highlands, grazing there without reser-
vation. This freedom, void of human interference,
shapes the personality of the horse. The young
horses grow up independent, learn how to treat
their environment and become more sensible – even
wiser. It is believed that horses brought up in these
circumstances become more attentive and intelli-
gent than horses brought up in narrow fields with
constant interaction with humans. The landscape
contributes to the sure-footedness of the horse and
it can be ridden in the mountains and tricky terrain, even at full gallop over uneven ground if necessary.

It was common practice in the country for all
horses not used in summer to be driven into the
highlands. This is still done in Skagafjördur and in
the Húnavatnssýsla counties in the northern part of
Iceland, although not as much as it used to be.

The protection of the grazing lands is an important consideration to Icelanders today as growth is
gradually being destroyed in the highlands, due in
some cases to the grazing of horses and sheep. All
breeders, however, still try to raise their horses in
wide fields without human interference if possible.

UPBRINGING AND TRAINING

The horse's training begins in its fourth and fifth
years. By the fourth year the horse should be handled with great care. Often, it receives only saddle
training. It is then allowed a period without any in-
struction at all.

Normally, training of young horses begins in the
latter part of the winter in order to allow them the
summer months to roam free. This, however, depends of course on the owner's approach. When a
horse is five years old its training becomes more intensive.

Training of horses has undergone changes in Iceland and the horses are now generally better trained
than in previous times. This is partly due to influence from abroad, where the training of horses has
become more established than in Iceland.

The change from being semi-wild in a herd to
undergoing training is enormous for the young
horse. This change must be taken into consideration
and everything must be done to make the transition
as smooth as possible. If the horse is overtrained it
can turn against its trainer. The horse has been
raised in a herd adhering to its pecking order and
rules and remaining outside most of the winter.

A thick mane and tail are prominent features of the Icelandic horse.

Those stallions considered unsuitable for breeding are castrated. This used to be carried out when they became two-year-olds. Now, however, they are castrated as yearlings as they are quicker to mature due to better quality of feed. Castrating is necessary to prevent them from impregnating the females. Two-year-olds are already fertile and must be kept segregated from the mares in the spring until they have been castrated.

Icelandic horse owners place considerable emphasis on young horses being brought up in a herd, without human interference. Promising young stallions are not castrated until they are judged at around four or five years old. Abroad, the horses are brought up with constant handling from people and it is more common there for horses to be kept as stallions for many years purely for riding. This is not common in Iceland unless the stallions are prized breeding horses continuing their training throughout the winter in an effort to keep them happier and fitter in the summer when they are turned loose with the mares.

When the training begins the horse is stabled. It must get used to humans and being handled. When the horse is no longer afraid of the trainer and begins to trust him or her, basic training begins. The horse's temperament dictates how easily it accepts its training and the dominance of the human. The Icelandic horse is considered to be quite adaptable and is relatively easy to train. They mature slowly and are not fully grown until they are six or seven

When riding horses are first taken indoors to begin their training, it is necessary to proceed carefully. They need time to adjust to the changes in their diet and the increase in their movement.

years old, which is old compared to most other breeds. Some horses are quick to mature physically but their minds do not always keep up with the development of their muscles. It is vital to be patient with those horses as the shock of being put to strenuous work can affect them mentally and they can turn into nervous, over-worked wrecks.

The Icelandic horse has a high longevity with many living to well over thirty years of age. To ensure its continuing health and endurance it is important not to work them too hard until they are eight years old. If they are well cared for, it is quite likely that good riding horses will maintain their quality until they are in their thirties.

The training usually takes place in the wintertime when the horses are stabled. Many are also trained during the summer and often the young horses are taken along on riding tours where they can run loose. This method strengthens them and educates them, both from being driven and led.

It has always been important to teach the young horse to be led before beginning its saddle-training and being ridden. Firstly, the young horses are taught to be led in hand beside the trainer. When they have learned this, they are tied to a halter fastened to a girth around another horse and taught to be led beside that horse. After they have become accustomed to this exercise they become easier hand horses, that is, the rider can easily lead the horse while mounted on another horse.

Horses are either trained by their owners or by

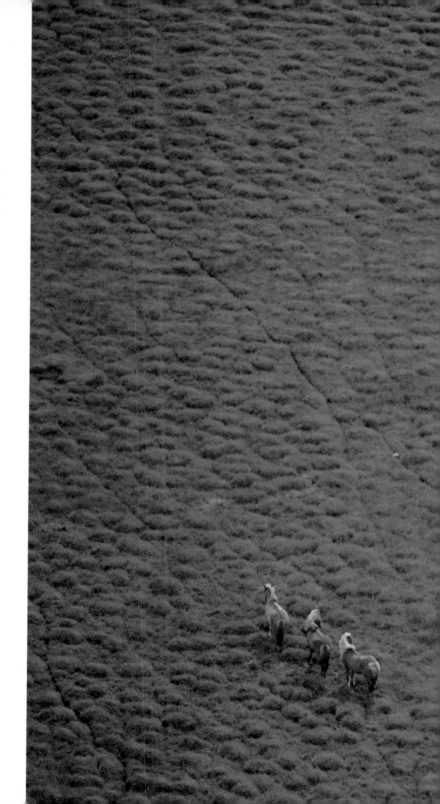

The peculiar tussocks of grass that appear widely in the Icelandic landscape have possibly contributed to the variety of the horse's gaits.

professional trainers. Often the owners teach the horse the basics, pacifying it and teaching it to be led. Having learned this the horse is then sent to a professional trainer for two or more months who trains it to be ridden.

Many people are fully employed as trainers in Iceland and their numbers are increasing following better education and greater experience. The growing number of pleasure riders also calls for more professionals.

To be a certified trainer one must go through intensive training and pass several tests. The Society of Professional Trainers in Iceland and the Agricultural College at Hólar educate and graduate professional trainers and riding instructors. The college at Hólar is particularly popular. Members of the Society of Professional Trainers hold seminars around the country throughout the year, with the demand for riding seminars growing. By building indoor riding halls in the stable areas of the bigger towns it is now possible to hold riding lessons in good facilities and without being dependent on the weather, which used to prevent many activities and events from taking place during the winter.

FOREIGN INFLUENCE

With the surge in the export of Icelandic horses, Icelandic riders were gradually introduced to the riding traditions of other nations. Many Icelandic riders accompanied horses to their new homes

The Icelandic horse has adapted surprisingly well to new environments where climate and conditions are very different than those which it was used to.

abroad where they learned new methods in training and riding, notably from the Germans. The Icelandic riders brought with them the Icelandic knowledge of the horse and showed how it should be ridden. Some of the new owners of the Icelandic horse were only used to riding the three-gaited foreign breeds and had to learn to ride the Icelandic horses.

Those riders that travelled abroad came home and gave riding seminars. Foreign riders also came to hold lectures and riding lessons. The new methods in riding and in training taught at these seminars awoke greater interest in the horse, and by around 1970 a new age had dawned on the Icelandic equestrian scene. Since then there have been rapid developments in riding and showing horses. As expected, many scorned the new methods, some, in the main, simply because they were foreign. More, however, were thrilled by the new approach and used what they thought was fitting and rejected what they felt was inappropriate for the Icelandic horse.

A Way of Life

When mechanisation started to make its mark on Icelandic agriculture in the fifties, man had to decide what to do with the horse. It took people a while to realise how valuable it was as a hobby. Horse enthusiasts founded riding clubs to support their interest. The first National Show, or Landsmót, was held at Thingvellir in 1950, where all of the best horses in the country were shown, starting an upturn in popularity in the process. This show was especially impressive as it became clear to spectators that the horse was a treasure of the island. Many have since said that that show confirmed that the horse had always had its place in the nation's heart.

The breeding of the Icelandic horse then became aimed at producing good riding horses. Riding became an important hobby for many living in towns. In these years many farmers had migrated to the towns, bringing their horses with them and building stables. These soon formed larger stabling areas and fields.

The National Association of Riding Clubs was founded in 1949, representing all riding clubs in the country. In the next few years the number of riding clubs had almost doubled and soon there were around fifty clubs with one in every county and large town.

In the Country and Towns

Fákur in Reykjavík, the oldest riding club in Iceland, was founded in 1922. By the middle of the century the club had built stables for its members where they could rent stalls for their horses. The club also held races, which became very popular, and a competition to find the best riding horse. The stables were on the outskirts of Reykjavík and soon became too small, requiring more boxes. A second stable area was constructed and today the headquarters of the club are based there in Víðidalur. The city already flanks this area but it remains the main stable area in Reykjavík, complete with riding halls and show grounds.

Stables have changed during the last few years and are today very well constructed, adhering strictly to specific standards. The horses require good housing with good air conditioning. It is a misunderstanding that the Icelandic horse doesn't need to be stabled; if it is not in training it can stay out all winter when provided with shelter and food, but if it is being ridden it must be stabled.

Reykjavík is probably the first capital in Europe to feature a huge stable area with thousands of horses within the city limits. Indeed, most towns in Iceland have stable areas.

Most of the urban planning in Iceland allows for stable areas on the outskirts of the towns and cities – it is as natural as making plans for a golf course!

Riding is highly social: people keep horses in companionship with other people: friends own stables together, ride together, graze their horses in the same pastures; while for many the highlight of every year is a summer riding tour.

The horses are trained for the tour the whole winter, initially with short riding trips every day which lengthen gradually. In the larger stable areas people share the morning feeding duties, returning to the stables after work to ride. By evening the stables are swarming with riders. As the days get longer so too do the rides and people start to make trips. The whole family is often together on such trips as the Icelandic horse is very family-friendly, if one can use that term. Children and teenagers enjoy the horse as much as their parents do.

In Iceland it is considered important that children be brought up around animals, and a special bond is often formed between a young rider and his or her horse. The Icelandic horse is so amiable and good-tempered that it can be trusted to carry young, inexperienced riders. Thus, the horse serves thousands in winter.

Many of the riding clubs operate a thorough programme of work for youths. Similar programmes exist at Icelandic horse clubs abroad. Children and teenagers are offered the possibility to go to riding seminars year round while all horse shows or meetings hold classes for young riders. As the years pass many of the young riders become very accomplished in the saddle, some better than many experienced riders.

Many elderly people enjoy riding as long as possible. Many look for a hobby after they retire and those involved with horses are very fortunate, as they are able to enjoy feeding the horses and taking care of them as much as riding. During the summer they join other riders on riding tours into the highlands.

Everyone is judged equally among the Icelandic riders – young or old, rich or poor. There is no class system in effect in the pastime that unites them.

Many farmers in Iceland breed horses. Some concentrate solely on rearing horses while others breed them as a hobby. Enthusiastic horse breeders can also be found in the cities. Farmers and so-called town breeders are closely associated. More often than not the same people buy from the same farmer: horses and hay for example. If the farmer lives near the town, he often accepts horses for grazing during the summer and autumn.

Around 20,000 to 30,000 people or 10% of the nation are thought to be involved with horses in Iceland. Horses demand a lot of attention from their owners, and as a consequence, it is not a hobby to be enjoyed only when one feels in the mood. Riding takes up a lot of time and money and it has been said that horsemanship is not so much a hobby but more a lifestyle. Maybe the reason is also to be found in the number of horses each interested family in Iceland owns, one city dweller having perhaps four horses with his family owning no fewer than eight or ten horses. If the situation is such, the interest is so huge that it is impossible to have other hobbies.

This also helps explain the increasing business ties between riders and farmers, from which everyone seems to be prospering.

GRAZING IN THE SUMMER

During the spring the horses should be fit enough for either competition or tours. By this time riding is possible almost twenty-four hours a day. Riding in the light of the midnight sun is both romantic and enchanting. In the stable areas a lot of activity is taking place and the tracks leading to and from the stables vibrate under the hoofs of the horses. This activity is happening everywhere in the country.

By the end of May and in the beginning of June the time has come to turn the horses out for grazing. Excitement always accompanies this decision, as many ride to the pastures in large groups with many horses. This of course only applies to those who have their horses grazing far away from the stable areas. Some have fields near the stables while others have to take their horses long distances. These trips to the fields are always good fun and they mark the beginning of the summer season.

In Reykjavík it is common to see groups of riders with herds of horses along the roads on their way to the summer fields. Such trips can take up to three or more days. Those who are too busy load their horses into trailers and transport them by vehicle to the fields.

It is great to ride to the summer pastures, espe-

cially if the destination remains the same. The horses, which almost always find their way, soon know where they are going. As they get nearer to their fields they become more and more alert as they know what to expect – freedom and green grass!

Their owners take care that this transition passes smoothly, as it can be dangerous to let horses who have been fed on hay the whole winter out into the fields of green grass without first adapting.

IN THE HIGHLANDS

Those fortunate enough to have their horses grazing nearby ride almost every day, or as often as possible in the summer months. Horses intended for competition are in training until their trainer presents them.

The summer is the best time of the year for many horsemen. During this season it is possible to ride wherever one likes, at any time during the day or night. People who have their horses further away use the weekends to ride and for many this is the main enjoyment of their life.

It is not long before preparations for the riding tours begin. During the winter, the summer tour is discussed and planned, whereas the shorter trips during that time of year are planned when the occasion arises. Special riding tracks are becoming more and more common, and resting places where people can change horses have been specially con-

It is magnificent to enjoy Icelandic nature – far away from the hustle and bustle of modern-day life.

structed. For longer trips the riders normally have hand horses, in some cases several. Depending on the distances involved, farmers visiting each other on horseback may take many horses along with them.

The summer riding tours are becoming increasingly popular in Iceland, and it is necessary to plan them in advance as it can be difficult to arrange sleeping accommodation and grazing for the horses without booking early. Highland tours are the most popular tours even though those in the lower country can be just as much fun.

It is necessary for the horses to be as fit as possible. Every rider on the tour requires several horses. Three horses are considered sufficient for each rider and it is important that the horses are no younger than six years old. All horses on such tours must be fully grown and fit.

The Icelandic horse is brought up in a hilly landscape and is thus at home in such surroundings. It is very sure-footed and can therefore travel at speed across uneven terrain, though it is important not to overwork it by going too fast or too far when the going is not good. The horses need to rest at regular intervals and it is best to change mounts often to conserve their strength.

Seasoned tour horses can easily endure the strain of hard work. They cross deep rivers with strong currents without hesitation; however, it is not recommended that riders unfamiliar with river-crossings do so without guidance. Normally thirty to fifty kilometers is considered enough for one day when the going for the horses is bad. It is recommended to keep the first days of the tour easy and short, increasing the distance on a gradual basis day by day as the horses become accustomed to the motion. If many travel together the spare horses are driven in a group, and they soon learn to line up one after another while moving along the tracks.

Riders crossing the highlands usually sleep over in mountain huts which these days are comfortable and well-provisioned. At many of these resting places it is possible to buy fodder for the horses, which are then fed in paddocks near the huts. Some huts also have adjoining stables which can come in handy when the weather is bad.

ORGANIZED RIDING TOURS

Organized riding tours have been developing for many years. In the beginning they were restricted to certain areas, but today companies specializing in riding tours are located throughout the country.

Highland tours are very popular, offering an extremely interesting perspective on travelling in the highlands on horseback exploring Icelandic nature. Foreign visitors represent an increasing share of the clientele, and the number of tourists coming to Iceland mainly because of the Icelandic horse is rising annually. In 1995, nine thousand people arrived in Iceland to participate in riding tours. The number of tourists on every tour varies but is normally around twenty. When there are so many riders the horses must at least number sixty. These tours are an adventure for all participating regardless of their nationality.

The distances covered in the first few days are short and it is vital that everyone acquires suitable horses. The riders travel in landscapes which cars are unable to access. By the evening the mobile kitchen vehicle has arrived with everything prepared in advance so that the riders can relax after a strenuous day in the saddle. Also during the evening the magnificent nature is discussed, and the horses are of course a constant source of conversation. Tourists often fall in love with a particular horse they ride and want to buy it at the end of the trip and export it to their homes abroad. All, however, fall in love with Iceland and all things Icelandic, and many return every year. These devotees of the Icelandic horses normally buy Icelandic clothing, with some even buying an Icelandic dog as well!

Many farmers offer horse rental and short tours – usually lasting anywhere from one hour up to a

number of days. Some foreign guests come every year to the same farmer for riding tours. What they seek from the horse is the smoothness of its gaits, its temperament and its friendly attitude towards humans. The experience of riding in tölt, the speciality of the Icelandic horse, enchants them and they claim never to have experienced anything similar before.

The longest riding tour ever to take place was in 1994. Around 1000 km were ridden across the highlands of Iceland in fourteen days of variable weather. The participants were pleased with the tour as well as with the changing conditions which only added a special flavour to the tour.

Today it is possible to participate in the herding or roundups of sheep and horses from the highlands – a unique experience for all who participate or observe. Foreign visitors enjoy the close contact with the farmers of the area, as well as the special atmosphere of the roundup itself where the Icelandic horse is employed in its natural role.

SELECTIVE BREEDING

The Icelandic horse has been isolated for 1100 years without the blood infusion of other breeds. The horses were brought up in harsh and merciless surroundings compared to other domestic animals, and they are quite wild when they are first broken in. Despite this wild upbringing they have partly been selectively bred for ages. Stud horses were well chosen and treasured in ancient times. These horses were protected and cherished, which was not the case with normal horses. Most of the horses were brought up in the freedom of the unfenced highlands. Stallions roamed the heaths with their group of mares, defending them from other stallions. Due to this freedom the horses bred freely, with many of the foals having an uncertain sire.

In the beginning of this century it was forbidden to turn stallions loose in the highlands even though these laws were not strictly adhered to, as they were allowed to be free on the lands of their owners.

Some farmers took better care of their horses and kept them together. Special bloodlines in the Icelandic breed were thus formed, consisting of horses who had some similar traits. Some of them produced better riding horses than other lines. The breeding has remained consistent during the last few decades, the old bloodlines have been mixed with others and almost everyone is interested in achieving better breeding.

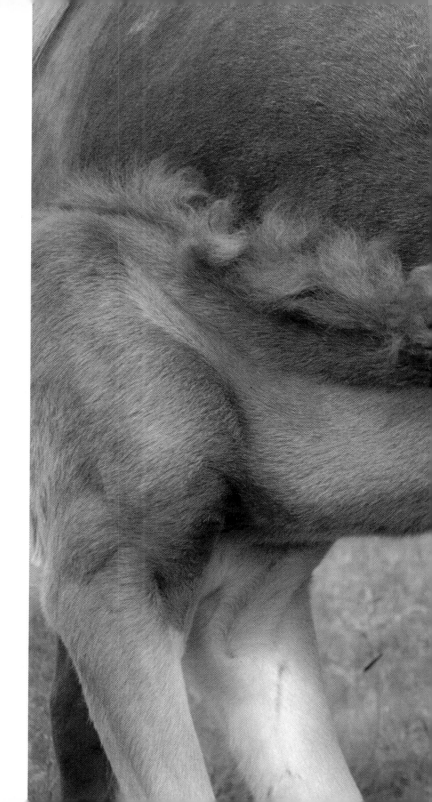

A new-born foal needs to suckle immediately after birth in order to survive.

THE LINES ARE OFTEN PARALLEL

It is difficult to discuss bloodlines within the Icelandic breed as the breeding was left mostly unattended to until this century, and the horses were isolated for ages. Most of the horses in Iceland are descended from a few individuals and are all more or less related.

One bloodline proved to be more influential than others: the Svadastadir line from Skagafjördur, the "bluegrass" country in the north of Iceland. Horses in Skagafjördur have been selectively bred longer than elsewhere in Iceland, and the Svadastadir horses were noted for their fine build as well as their being good riding horses with quality gaits. The Svadastadir line, however, soon split into several other lines, the most famous being the Kolkuóss line in Skagafjördur.

The most prominent breeder in Skagafjördur these days is Sveinn Gudmundsson in Saudárkrókur. Horses descended from his stock dominate the Icelandic horse breeding scene.

Another sub-line of Svadastadir is the bloodline of the horses from Kirkjubær in Rangárvellir. There, horses have been selectively bred for 60 years with the goal of breeding chestnut horses, with a blaze, good movements and good temperament, and quality gaits.

When discussing breeding from point of origin it is impossible not to mention the horses from

44

Promising young stallions stepping like two professional dancers.

Hornafjördur. For ages these horses have been more or less isolated from horses in other parts of the country. The landscape in the eastern part of Iceland is dominated by glacial rivers and all travelling was difficult for riders and horses until the rivers were bridged. These horses were characterized by their strength and toughness. They were often thought to be quite difficult to ride because of their stubbornness and quick tempers, yet they grew up crossing glacial rivers safely with their sharp instincts leading the way. These good "water-horses" as they were called were valuable, as they were strong and reliable.

At one time stallions of this bloodline became quite popular, but due to their inconsiderable numbers they were too heavily interbred, and today only a few breeders breed these horses. Their influence on the blood stock is now dwindling.

BREEDING GOALS NOW AND THEN

Horse breeding today is built on well-bred mares which have received excellent judging. The number of qualified mares increases every year thanks to the availability of a rising number of quality stallions, better training and showing. The number of well-bred and excellent stallions is high, indicating that the Icelandic breeders have done their homework during the past few years. In the southern part of Iceland where more than 100 stallions were in training in 1996, only a handful will be judged good enough and catch the eye of the critical spectators attending the breeding shows.

It is interesting to compare the goals the horse breeding advisor to Iceland Gunnar Bjarnason revealed in a speech in 1951, to those used today: "As the need for ploughing horses or heavy draught horses is almost non-existent today it is my belief that the attitude towards breeding must change from what it was 10-15 years ago. The heavy horse used for farming is history. Today we need more than ever before strong, willing, easy-to-ride and most of all nicely tempered horses. This can easily go along with breeding good riding horses. It is therefore my belief that the common breeding goal should be breeding versatile horses for riding, transportation and working with the hay, which also have good nerves and good temperament. These horses would also be suitable for exportation if the need arises in the future.... The nicely tempered, strong, willing and agile riding horse is what we need and should be breeding, to serve both the pleasure riders and the farmers. The high-tempered, quality-gaited horses will be used for experienced riders but the others can be versatile horses for all." (Gunnar Bjarnason: *Ættbók og Saga II*, p. 39.)

GOOD TÖLT AND WILLINGNESS

It can be difficult to decide which type of horse will suit the masses. People's needs, abilities and interests are different and therefore it can be difficult to choose. The Icelandic breed has several types of horses and everyone has their own favourite. It is, however, relatively easy to describe how the horse must be to fulfill the breeding judges' image of the perfect Icelandic horse.

The breeding aims towards excellence; goals are made and judgements are constructed in view of those goals. Conformation and gaits are judged separately, with seven individual features graded in each (fourteen all in all), and the average of the conformation grade and the gait grade becomes the grade of the horse. Each individual grade, such as the grade for head, carries its own weight on the average judgement according to its importance for the horse. From these weights it is easy to see which trait is most sought after.

In the conformation judgement, neck and shoulders carry the highest weight, which means that breeders want better necks and shoulders, which enable the horse to carry itself more gracefully, for example in the tölt. An excellent neck should be long, thin and fine, enabling a good arch of the head. The neck must be highly raised and must also be well defined from the withers, which should be high, well shaped, with sloping shoulders.

The breeding goal is to make the front of the horse as light and fine as possible since the Icelandic horse has a rather short and thick neck compared to other horse breeds. The grade for legs and their straightness also carries a lot of weight, as the Ice-landic horse is renowned for strong and healthy legs. It is one trait breeders do not want to see disappear.

In view of gaits the goal is as before to breed an excellent riding horse (gæðingur). To reach that goal, traits such as temperament and character are important as they enable the rider to make as much of the gaits of each individual as possible. The horse should be strong, with a good temperament and quality gaits. The speciality of the Icelandic horse lies in the quality of the gaits and an amiable character.

The seven features which the gaits and the ridability of the horse are judged by also carry different weighting, depending on their importance. The tölt carries the most, as the grade for tölt is multiplied by 20, which is almost double the weight for any other gait. The tölt is judged both in slow gait and in more speed. The best tölt should feature a clear-beat, the horse should have large steps, high leg action and suppleness in changes of speed. The better the grades the stallions and mares achieve for tölt, the better they should be for breeding.

The pace comes next to tölt in terms of weight, and is multiplied by 12. Not all horses have pace worth showing but it is considered good for the tölt if the horse has some pace which can then contribute to a better tölt. Therefore, it is thought that without breeding for pace the tölt would soon be lost.

Temperament also carries a high weighting or 10, as it is essential for a quality-gaited horse to have the right attitude for using its gaits. The temperament should be high but flexible and the horse must not try to take control of the rider, that is take off with its rider.

Simply put, the breeding goal today is to breed a horse with a fine, long and well-carried neck on good legs and hoofs. The horse must have excellent tölt, good pace and trot, a good but flexible temperament and excellent character: in short a five-gaited, beautiful and excellent riding horse.

THE BLUP-EVALUATION

In 1986 a new evaluation for breeding horses was introduced to Icelandic breeders. This new evaluation, named BLUP (Best Linear Unbiased Prediction) is constructed of the judgement of the horse and its lineage. Fourteen features are evaluated and points are given for each feature. One hundred points is average, and from this evaluation of the features an average grade is made. Breeding predictions for untrained horses are made on the basis of their parents' evaluations, and when the offspring is judged its grades will affect the grades of its parents. Stallions are split into three groups: stallions with more than 50 judged offspring, stallions with 15-49 judged offspring, and stallions with fewer than 15 judged offspring. If a stallion attains more than 125 points with 50 or more judged offspring he receives an honorary prize for offspring. A stallion with 15-49 judged offspring and 125 points, or a stallion with more than 30 judged offspring and 120 points, receives first prize for offspring. Correc-

tions on these predictions are made yearly involving complicated computer calculations.

This system is the basis for choosing stallions suitable for breeding. When stallions are exported it depends on their BLUP-points whether local breeders have first options on buying them.

All judged mares are also evaluated as individuals. Mares with more than 120 points for at least five offspring receive an honorary prize for offspring and mares with 115 points and at least four offspring receive first prize for offspring.

This system enables the breeder to see which traits appear to be inherited both in conformation and in gaits, and he can then breed horses on that basis.

A HUGE AMOUNT OF WORK

Horse breeding in Iceland is based on a few basic operations. It begins with the local horse breeding associations which have been very influential in the last few decades. Iceland is split into four districts, south, north, west and east, and in each district there is one or more horse breeding association. Within the associations, divisions or clubs work in smaller areas or counties. The horse breeding associations are then all united in the national Horse Breeding Association of Iceland. Each association is independent and their main purpose is to enable the breeders in each district easy access to good stallions. In many cases the associations jointly buy expensive stallions, while others are rented from individuals or other associations or syndicates. This enables individual breeders to bring their mares to prized stallions for a moderate fee.

The horse breeding associations represent the individual breeders who form them in close co-ordination with the Farmers' Association of Iceland. The Farmers' Association employs horse breeding advisors who take care of all registrations involving horse breeding, judging and counselling.

The development has been such that the number of stallions that have been awarded the desired first prize has increased in close accordance with improvements in breeding and training. Most of the stallions are individually owned in the beginning. If the stallion turns out to be exceptionally good and attracts a lot of attention at the big horse meetings, the owner can sell it to the horse breeding associations if they are interested or syndicate it privately. Some owners, of course, prefer to own the stallions themselves, while some are sold abroad and exported.

BREEDING SHOWS

Every spring breeding shows are held around the country where mares and stallions are individually judged for conformation and gaits. County shows are held for horses from that particular county, and the best horses in the country are then shown and judged again at the big meetings – District Shows (Fjórdungsmót) or National Shows (Landsmót).

From 1950 National Shows have been held every fourth year, and in between District Shows are held, one every year, although only every fourth year in each district. Beginning in the year 2000 National Shows will be held every second year and the District Shows will cease to function.

From the beginning these big horse shows were held in co-operation with the National Association of Riding Clubs and the Farmers' Association, which handles all breeding matters. Breeding horses are judged and shown in these meetings and attract a larger audience than any other feature of these meetings. There, the best stud horses in the country are presented, as individuals, or with offspring, shown for a first or an honorary prize.

Stud horses have to qualify for the big meetings in preliminary judging and if the horse has reached a certain average grade it can be presented at a District Show or at the National Show. The horse breeding advisors of the Farmers' Association head the judging committees and the judgements are always expectantly awaited, first to see if the horse has qualified, then at the big show to see if it has improved and whether it will be among the top horses.

Classes are held for four-year-olds, five-year-olds, and horses six years old and older, besides the classes held for horses shown with offspring.

Foreign visitors attend in their thousands to watch the National Show and the bigger District Shows to see the best horses of Iceland and the offspring of the famous stallions. They also come to view horses from individual breeders.

IN COMPETITION – MAKING THEIR MARKS

What distinguishes the Icelandic horse from most other horse breeds are the two special gaits, tölt and pace. Because of these gaits a special competition, gæðingakeppni, has developed where the riding ability and the quality of the horse are judged. The competition is split into two classes, the B-class for four-gaited horses who show walk, trot, canter and tölt, and the A-class for five-gaited horses who in addition to the four gaits also show pace. The horses must have all gaits clear-beat with good rhythm and they are also given marks for willingness and beauty under the saddle/rider. The riding clubs in Iceland all hold local meetings in gæðingakeppni, where races and often equestrian sports are a part of the programme. The sport events are similar to the gæðingakeppni but more demands are made on the rider and his riding of the horse in the gaits.

The meetings generating the most excitement are the District Shows and the National Show as discussed in the chapter on stud horses. At these meetings the best horses in each district or in the whole country are presented – the best gæðingar (riding horses) and the best stud horses which have all had to qualify in the preliminary meetings.

The High Point of Horsemanship

The National Show is the outdoor event that attracts the most spectators in Iceland. People come in hordes from every part of the country to watch the best Icelandic horses in the land compete.

Horse competitions have been with the nation from early settlement. At that time a horse's endurance and swiftness was tested in races. Stallions were also made to fight until one of them lay dead. It was a matter of honour to have a good fighting stallion and many sagas tell of stallion fights. One such fight takes place in one of the most famous sagas, *Brennu-Njálssaga*, when the sons of Starkadur spurred their stallion on against the stallion of Gunnar from Hlídarendi beneath the mountain of Thríhyrningur. Those who lost fights like this often sought revenge, such was the ambition in those days.

Races were popular and were often the highlight of public meetings where horses were tested against each other in gallop and pace. *Landnáma*, which tells the story of the early settlers in Iceland, carries a story of the settler Thórir Dúfunef who settled at the farm Flugumýri in Skagafjördur. He bought a mare he had never seen that had escaped from the ship she came to Iceland on. He found her eventually and named her Fluga and she became the fastest horse of all. A sorcerer named Örn waited once for Thórir when he was riding to the Althing and dared Thórir to race against him, as

Örn had a very good horse. They bet in silver coins, and when they came to even grounds, later called Dúfunefsstadur, the race began. The difference in the quality and swiftness of the horses was such that when Thórir had returned and was on the way back he met with Örn who was only halfway through. Örn could not bear losing and committed suicide by the mountain which is now named after him, Arnarfell. Fluga was left on the race track as she was "out of breath" and when Thórir returned from the Althing he found a grey stallion beside Fluga, now in foal to this stallion. Their offspring was Eidfaxi who was later sold to Norway where he became a famous fighter. This is the oldest story of a horse race in Iceland.

The local horse shows are normally celebratory occasions for those participating and observing. People come riding to the meeting with their best horses and competitions are held in almost all disciplines. It is always an honour to own the best horses and when the gædingakeppni is over, the races begin.

The first National Show in Iceland was held in the summer of 1950, a year after the foundation of the National Association of Riding Clubs in Iceland. It took place amidst the historic setting of Thingvellir. All the riding clubs in Iceland had the right to send teams to the meeting and such is still the custom today. The number of representatives from each club depends on the number of members in that individual club and thus horses and riders from all parts of the country have the opportunity to compete against each other.

GREAT EXPECTATIONS

The number of members in the individual club determines how many riders that club may send to a National Show or a District Show. The expectations are thus great and the tension is palpable. The hopeful have trained their horses diligently for months or years and await the results expectantly. It is considered a great achievement both for riders and breeders, who often spend a lot of money for that purpose, to earn the right to compete or show their horses at these big meetings, as it is a huge advertisement. The best riders are fought over by prominent breeders and many of the riders are in such demand that they can choose only the best horses. The National Shows are today almost wholly made up of professionals.

It is not the same to show a breeding horse as to show a riding horse. In the breeding judgements the horse is also judged for its conformation and must therefore look as good as possible.

The quality of these meetings has been increasing steadily and the facilities have changed much to keep up with the demands of interested spectators who come in considerable numbers to watch good horses and brilliant riders.

To qualify as a judge in the riding horse contest the individual must have completed a course in judging, held by the Judging Committee of the National Association of Riding Clubs, and passed a strict test. These judges have to judge some competitions every year to keep their licence. Experienced judges can then take a test to become a national judge. Only national judges can judge at National Shows. Seminars for judges are held every year where the judges compare their notes and develop co-ordination. Before every big meeting a group of judges is selected and that group judges some smaller meetings before they judge the big meeting to improve this co-ordination between them. When judging the gædingakeppni the grades are shown on special placards. Each judge judges individually and puts the grades on the placards after the horse has completed the test. The judge has an assistant who is also a judge. This procedure is also used by the Icelandic Equestrian Association (HÍS).

The National Show competitions have been held alternately in the north and in the south and are one of the most popular events in Iceland. They are certainly an event worth experiencing.

Attendance at these meetings has been increasing and the events are getting larger and larger. At the first National Show there were only classes for adults, but today children and young riders have classes of their own. Normally an open tölt event is also held at the National Show and at races. The tölt event is always one of the highlights of the meeting, where the best tölters in Iceland compete for the gold.

The National Shows usually take five days and every day is filled with events of all sorts such as rides, barbeques and dances. Many people camp by the show grounds, and the camping grounds are lively. People from all over the country come and many ride for a few days to the meeting. No other event in Iceland attracts as many foreign visitors as these meetings, which are the true festivals of the Icelandic horsemen.

In all horse shows in Iceland, children, youngsters and since 1996 young riders have their own classes. In the classes for children and youngsters points are given for seat and gaits, each section making up a half of the average grade. In the class for young riders the same rules apply as for adults, it is a gæðingakeppni for young riders where only the horse is judged.

The mounts of the younger riders are getting better every year and so is their riding ability. The competition is fierce and the riders are expected to do well. The same rules apply for their attendance at District Shows or National Shows as for adults,

The spectators all have their own
opinions, having judged each horse
for themselves.

and are based on the number of members in their club.

EQUESTRIAN EVENTS

When Icelanders were introduced to riding abroad, their interest for horse sports awakened. In the so-called equestrian events, the rider is judged as well as his horse and their joint grade is based on the ability of the rider to show the horse to its best advantage. In gædingakeppni it is different, as there the best riding horse is being sought after. Shortly after the National Association of Riding Clubs (LH) was established the interest in equestrian events increased and special sport divisions were founded within the riding clubs. In 1970 the first European Championships for Icelandic horses were held and in their wake a special sport council was founded within LH to hold Icelandic Championships annually in the equestrian events. A huge interest mounted in getting the sport council into the public sports system, the Icelandic Sport Federation (ÍSÍ).

In 1977 the first equestrian sport meeting was held in Reykjavík, a sort of introductory meeting.

This led to the founding of the Icelandic Equestrian Association (HÍS) in 1989, an independent association within ÍSÍ. The sport divisions within the riding clubs are members of HÍS, which handles all affairs concerning the equestrian sport events, such as competition, education etc. HÍS handles the participation of the Icelandic team in the World Championships mentioned in the chapter on the Icelandic horse abroad.

This development can be traced to the foundation of Félag Tamningamanna (FT), the Society of Professional Trainers, in 1970, which has been active in everything concerning competition and training for the Icelandic horse. FT is a member organization of LH but works independently. It has educated trainers and published teaching material, and given tests for trainers. The work carried out by FT has caused more participation in the equestrian sport events and more professionalism in training horses.

As an example of the equestrian sport events, the tölt-competition can be described. The marks given in the tölt-competition are built on the harmony between horse and rider. It is not always so that the best tölter will win; the rider who with his horse can perform the exercises best will win the tölt event. The main emphasis is on three main features: slow tölt, speed changes in tölt, and fast tölt. The slow tölt must not be too slow and the beat must be a clear four-beat, the speed changes must be performed correctly at exact places of the oval track where the horse is asked to increase the speed from slow tölt to medium tölt and then slow down into slow tölt again. The fast tölt must be performed with an even fast speed and always correct four-beat – the track being an oval 250 m long.

This is the same in other events of the sport except in pace which is of course performed on a straight pace track with the demands on the rider to make the best of the horse's gaits in a precise and controlled performance. In pace test the horse should begin in tölt, go into canter, from canter to flying pace and then slow down in tölt down to walk. The rider is judged for his riding ability.

The equestrian sport events are getting more and more popular, as they are fascinating events demanding intense training of both horse and rider. The dressage is a part of the events as well as show jumping. These events are the only ones based on foreign models. The interest for these two disciplines is not as great as for the gait disciplines but all good riders acknowledge that dressage is a basis for the suppleness of the trained horse. Show jumping, however, is a discipline which does not suit the Icelandic horse as well as it suits the foreign breeds – and it can never compete against those breeds in this area.

Every summer the Icelandic Championships in equestrian sport events are held, besides all the smaller meetings held by the individual sport divisions.

TREADING ON FOREIGN GROUND

Many of those living outside Iceland are under the misapprehension that the Icelandic horse is only suitable for carrying children. Some even think that it is tantamount to animal abuse to see adults weighing up to 100 kg or more riding these horses at full speed. Abroad, the Icelandic horse is certainly a lot different from the horses most riders are used to – such as the long-legged, elegant thoroughbreds often seen being trained in the woods or in riding halls. The Icelandic horse – small, short-legged, and furry in winters, is perhaps not very attractive to riders used to the sleeker, well-groomed animals mentioned above.

Experience, however, has revealed that as soon as the doubtful riders have been properly introduced to the breed, they seem to find something which changes their minds, and many riders in Europe and in North America have become smitten with the Icelandic horse. The popularity of the Icelandic horse is increasing annually and today there are more Icelandic horses abroad than in Iceland. Thousands of people now enjoy the special qualities of the horse and devote all their spare time to being around them. A special culture has evolved wherever the Icelandic horse has settled, and owners have formed special bonds with other Icelandic horse owners through their mutual interest.

Many prize-winning stallions have been sold to owners abroad and are in high demand.

WIDESPREAD PROMOTION

After 1950 Gunnar Bjarnason, the then horse breeding advisor to the Farmers' Association, began encouraging the breeding of ponies in Europe. He had done an enormous amount of work in promoting the Icelandic horse abroad and his work started to snowball. Bjarnason thought it was high time that pony breeders in Europe formed an association, something they eventually did in February 1951. Soon it became clear that the Icelandic horse did not belong among the pony breeds, as despite its smallness it was more like a large horse.

In these years the exportation of Icelandic horses increased on an annual basis. Germany was the main importer of Icelandic horses and remains so to this day. Icelandic breeders soon realised that the horse needed promoting in other countries and soon Scandinavia, the Netherlands, Belgium, Switzerland and Austria became countries importing horses from Iceland. Other countries followed in their wake and the interest seems to be continually growing.

The Icelandic horse has always enjoyed wide promotion from Icelanders as well as owners and breeders abroad. Many have invested substantial amounts of money in breeding and selling horses and thus promote the horse wherever possible. Every year numerous shows are held all over Europe and North America, where the Icelandic horse is fast becoming a permanent fixture among the other breeds.

One show, however, has had the most impact on

the promotion of the Icelandic horse, the Equitana show held in Essen, Germany every second year. This huge horse show features all breeds, with the Icelandic horse a popular fixture. The event attracts hundreds of thousands of enthusiasts.

In the summer of 1996 the first Equitana show was held in the USA and introduced the Icelandic horse. Such shows are in the main attended by horse enthusiasts and they offer enormous potential for increasing the awareness of the animal. Horsemen introduced to the Icelandic horse at shows such as these display interest in the small horse with its willingness, toughness, gaits and temperament. They recognise its suitability for the public and in that respect the shows are considered an important marketing outlet.

In this context it should be mentioned that wherever the Icelandic horse has settled, magazines covering the breed are being published, and in some countries more than one. These magazines are of good quality and many are published monthly. The Icelandic horse is therefore not only presented live but also in words and pictures.

COMMUNICATIONS

It is not sufficient just to export the horses; people must be taught how to take care of them and enjoy them. In the 1960s Icelandic trainers began to be employed abroad, teaching people the correct way to ride the horse. They held riding seminars as well as bringing horses with them. Many of those trainers settled abroad, founded training centers and today train, teach, breed and sell the Icelandic horse.

This development has increased ever since and has contributed towards the rise in demand for Icelandic horses as well as establishing ties with the home country for the owners of the horses.

The relationship between Icelandic riders and foreign enthusiasts is diverse. Many young riders, especially from northern Europe, come to Iceland to work with the Icelandic horse while others come to study at the Agricultural College in Hólar which offers courses in training and horsemanship. Every summer many tourists come to Iceland for the express purpose of travelling on horseback, experiencing the horse in its natural surroundings as well as meeting the people involved with horses in Iceland.

These international relations, which include Icelandic riders staying among their colleagues abroad, have taught Icelanders much. There is no question that these communications have left their mark on the development of Icelandic horsemanship and riding, and have enabled foreign riders to get a better grip on their subject.

BREEDING ABROAD

The increased interest in the Icelandic horse abroad soon arrived at the point where foreign owners wanted to breed the horse by themselves and began searching for possible stud horses.

But the plans to export stallions met with resistance among Icelandic breeders. Many of them claimed that if stallions were exported the Icelandic exporting market would crash as other nations would take over the breeding of the Icelandic horse.

Some positive and farsighted men claimed, however, that the export of stallions would only increase the export of geldings. Among those was the horse breeding advisor Gunnar Bjarnason. He pointed out that everywhere live stock was transported between countries, breeding animals were also included. To be involved in breeding would only fire the interest which would soon spread. Bjarnason's judgement has been found to be correct as even though thousands of stud horses are now abroad, the export of horses continues to increase. Foreign breeding is restricted in countries like the Netherlands, Belgium and Switzerland, by lack of space as the land is considered insufficient to support many horses. Germany, however, has more land and there breeding is often conducted on a large scale.

In Scandinavia, the Danes and the Swedish are the largest breeders and are currently experiencing an upswing. The interest in Norway for the Icelandic horse is huge, while Finland has a shorter history, only beginning to import horses in 1980.

Today prized stallions and brood mares are exported from Iceland although the best are kept at home whenever possible. The fact that Iceland is the home country, the number of horses and the fact that the best are not exported have contributed to the undisputed lead Iceland maintains in breeding affairs, although many foreigners have been breeding good horses for quite a long time.

WORLDWIDE

It soon became clear, as the Icelandic horse became more widely known abroad, that it could not be classified as a pony. Its special gaits and diversity called for advanced riding, while its caretaking and connections to its home country united its owners in a special group. These facts soon called for an association of Icelandic horse owners.

In Europe the International Federation of Icelandic Horse Associations, FEIF (Föderation Europaischer Islandpferde Freunde), was founded in 1969. Earlier, riding clubs and national associations had been founded in several countries and championships for Icelandic horses were held. Abroad, as in Iceland, small riding clubs formed associations in the individual countries.

FEIF handles competition and breeding affairs. Rules for competition and for the European Championships held every second year were agreed upon and the first European Championships for Icelandic horses were held in Aegiedienberg, Germany in 1970, twenty years after the first National Show was held in Iceland. After the USA and Canada joined FEIF these championships were re-named World Championships. The Canadians have competed in the World Championships since 1985 and the US since 1989.

These championships are held every second year in individual countries in Europe, except Iceland, as no horse can ever return to Iceland due to an importation ban concerning animals. Horses representing the Icelandic team must all be sold following the competition. The other national teams can have the same horses competing on their behalf for many championships, and many of the former horses of the Icelandic team have later represented another country at later championships.

The events of the World Championships are the equestrian events: tölt, four-gait, five-gait, pace test, 250m pace and dressage. In the championships all the best riders of the participating countries, those who have earned their place on their national teams, compete against each other. The competitions are fierce and the excitement is palpable among the thousands of spectators.

One of the facts which make the Championships so much fun is the opportunity to meet Icelandic horse enthusiasts from at least 20 countries. Icelanders are just as interested in attending these and other multinational meetings such as the Nordic Championships. Icelanders consider it valuable to meet people abroad, hopefully enabling them to sell more horses. These championships have an influence on riding, both among Icelanders and their foreign friends.

Stud horses are also judged at these championships, although the countries can only send breeding horses born in that individual country to compete on their behalf.

Within FEIF the main emphasis is on youth work, and this aspect has been given more stress every year. Special youth championships are held, and youth camps are run in some European countries. At these meetings the youth of participating FEIF countries meet their peers and compete against each other.

Mutual visits involving teenagers from different countries are popular, both in groups and individually. Icelandic teenagers are sought after to work abroad in summer at the horse farms where Icelandic horses are bred and trained. It is also common that young people from Europe or the USA travel to Iceland to work with horses for a period of time.

SETTLEMENT IN AMERICA

The Icelandic horse caused a lot of attention when it was among the participants in the Great American Horse Race, a ride across the USA held to commemorate the country's 200-year anniversary in 1976. Due to the influence of legendary Icelandic horse enthusiasts in Germany, Austria and Switzerland, it was decided that the Icelandic horse would take part in the ride.

In this great endurance ride many breeds such as Arabians, Quarter Horses, Appaloosas, Paso Finos

and Peruvian Pasos and Russian Orlov trotters as well as numerous mixtures and mules participated. This was not a contest of the best riding horse but an endurance ride for strong and fit horses. The Icelandic breed was of course the smallest horse but proved its worth. The ride took more than three months, with daily riding for 60-65 km and the Icelandic horses came in among the first. This incredible performance of the small but fit horse caused a sensation.

Lately, the export of Icelandic horses to the USA and Canada has seen an increase, and it looks as if the Icelandic horse is there to stay. But America is huge and it will take a long time for the Icelandic horse to become established, as distances are great. However, small groups of riders exchanging knowledge and competing together are beginning to form, and as soon as the competition involving Icelandic horses is as recognized as it is in Europe it can be expected that more and more horses will be imported.

Icelanders are aware of the need to introduce interested parties to correct methods of riding and taking care of the Icelandic horse. Promotion and education is thus very important, as if it is correctly carried out the Icelandic horse will win the market by itself.

A Bright Future

No one could have imagined in 1950 how popular the Icelandic horse would become in its home country and abroad. The experience of the last decades has taught us that the more advanced technology became, the more the popularity of the Icelandic horse grew.

Today the working population has more time off and it chooses to spend that time returning to nature, enjoying the outdoor life, and relaxing far away from the noise and speed of the technology-filled day. The horse fulfills this need for relaxation and leisure in the embrace of nature, and perhaps no horse as much as the Icelandic horse.

The horse has always been honoured among the Icelandic nation, and was named the "truest servant" for centuries. Even if its importance dwindled temporarily as machines took over its role, the nation soon missed it. Its star shone again and a new role was found for it, a role it will continue to fill in the future, both at home and abroad.

Icelanders are thought to have the oldest parliament in the world. The Althing was founded by the Icelandic nation at Thingvellir around 930 AD. People rode to the Althing from all parts of the country once a year. Thingvellir hosted the first National Show in 1950, and the hoof prints can still be seen in the old paths leading to Thingvellir; they are still being used by riders today. Deep tracks have been marked in the grass lands and in the lava, often many side by side. As modern man rides these tracks he is transported back through history and in tune with long-gone generations. There he listens to the "hum of the centuries" as a well-known Icelandic author once wrote.

In the past men came to the Althing on their own, a few together, or in big parties. Then men and horses were counted in hundreds and the earth vibrated under the hoofs.

Today, riding tours across the highlands are so popular that some groups number up to 30 riders and around 100 horses. It is sometimes as if time has stood still.

The final words of this book feature a quote from Broddi Jóhannesson from his book *Faxi* published in 1945. They reveal a true picture of the relationship between the horse and the nation over the past thousand years or so:

"The wealth of humans is measured in how often they say yes to living. Everything which inspires their love increases their wealth. Even if the Icelandic people were often hard on their horses they always loved them and never did the horses cause their hatred. It is obvious that many of the main moments in the history of Iceland would never have happened without the horse; it has also taken part in the pleasures of every child in this country for more than ten centuries. This should be remembered by our descendants even if the horse were to disappear." (P. 440)

The horse will not disappear as long as there is a nation living in Iceland. More and more Icelanders understand its role in our modern society and the necessity to take care of it as well as of the nature which has been entrusted to us from one generation to another.